Why I'm a
PRETRIBULATIONAL
PREMILLENNIALIST

and Why You Should Be, Too

RANDY WHITE

Copyright © 2017 Randy White
Cover and Illustration: Leonardo Costa
Cover and Illustrations © 2017 DispensationalPublishing House, Inc.

All rights reserved. This book or any portion thereof may not be reproduced or used in any manner whatsoever without the express written permission of the publisher except for the use of brief quotations in a book review.

All Scripture quotations, unless otherwise indicated,
are taken from the New King James Version®.
Copyright © 1982 by Thomas Nelson. Used by permission. All rights reserved.

Printed in the United States of America
First Edition, First Printing, 2017
ISBN: 978-1-945774-11-9

DispensationalPublishing House, Inc.
PO Box 3181, Taos, NM 87571

www.dispensationalpublishing.com

Orders by U.S. trade bookstores and wholesalers. Please contact the publisher:
Tel: (844) 321-4202

1 2 3 4 5 6 7 8 9 10

*To Shelley, who has encouraged and blessed me
in all of my theological journeys.*

TABLE OF CONTENTS

INTRODUCTION 7
  Defining the Terminology of Eschatology 8
  Representing the Views 10

PRELIMINARY QUESTIONS ON PRETRULATIONISM 13
  When Will the Rapture Occur? 13
  Graphically Representing the Current Views on Rapture 15
  Are the Rapture and the Second Coming the Same Thing? 18
  Is the Second Coming Imminent? 19
  Requirements for the Second Coming 22
  Is the Rapture Imminent? 23
  Is the Second Coming Visible? 24
  Is the Rapture Visible? 25
  Where Will the People of God Gather At His Return? 26
  Will the Rapture Really Occur? 29

MY THEOLOGICAL JOURNEY 33

MORE QUESTIONS ABOUT PRETRIBULATIONISM 37

What is The Day of the Lord? 37

What Has to Happen Before the Day of the Lord Occurs?..39

Has a "Falling Away" Occurred? 40

Has the "Man of Sin" Been Revealed?......................42

Why I Believe in Pretribulationism.........................43

CONCLUSION 47

INTRODUCTION

As a premillennialist, I believe Christ will come back before the kingdom of God is established on this earth.

As a pretribulational premillennialist, I believe Christians will be raptured *before* the great tribulation which is prophesied in the Old Testament and fully described in the book of Revelation.

Before delving into my change from a one-time *post*tribulational premillennialist, let's get clear on some more terminology. These are important terms to understand as we wade through why right belief about the end times matters today.

Defining the Terminology of Eschatology

As you likely already know from words like theology and sociology, "ology" simply means "the study of." "Escha" comes from the Greek word for "last." So, if we put them together, eschatology means "the study of the last," i.e. the study of the end times.

In Christian belief, the end times may be ahead of us, or we may even be living in the end times right now. The end times include *the great tribulation*, a future seven-year period in which God's wrath is poured on the nations and the Jewish people are brought to a point of recognition of Jesus as Messiah. Christians differ on their beliefs about the end times. This short book aims to reveal proper biblical thinking about the end of days. But there's more terminology we need to clarify so that we're all on the same page.

While some people reject a literal interpretation, a *millennium* is a thousand years. I believe that the millennium is the Kingdom of God, in which Jesus Christ reigns on earth for that one thousand years, followed by the New Heaven, the New Earth, and New Jerusalem. All Christians believe that Christ will return. However, they differ on *when* they think he'll return.

- If you believe that Christ will return *before* the millennium begins, you're a *premillennialist*, like me.

- If you believe that Christ will return *after* the millennium ends, you're a *postmillennialist*.

- If you believe that Christ will return *during* the millennium and that we've been living in the millennium since Pentecost, or that there's no defined millennium, you're an *amillennialist*.

What do postmillennialists and amillennialists have in common? You'll never hear a sermon focused on the rapture from either. Neither group has a significant rapture theology because they believe the rapture is a minor event or is symbolic of some other event that has or will take place. In other words, if you're talking with someone who believes that the rapture will happen in a literal and significant way, you're certainly talking to a premillennialist.

Representing the Views

For most of us, a graphical representation of the millennial views will help us understand the differences. In the charts that follow, the major components of each chart are given from the cross through the second coming. Some charts contain a rapture and the Tribulation while others do not. This is because some millennial views have little or no place for these two events. The major difference of the views is the placement of the millennium in relation to the Second Coming.

INTRODUCTION • 11

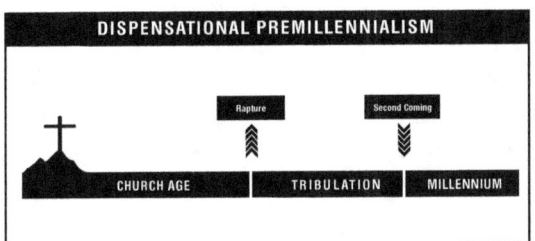

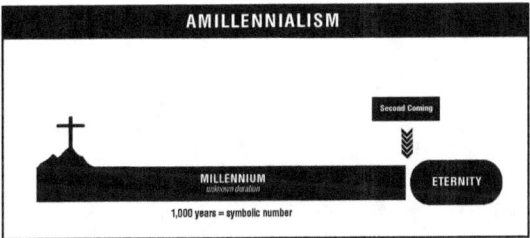

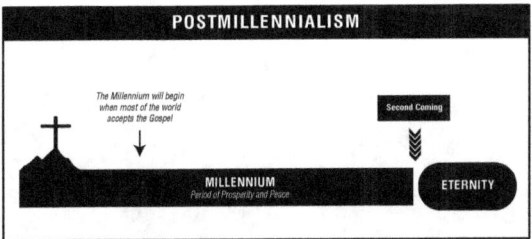

CHAPTER 1

PRELIMINARY QUESTIONS ON PRETRULATIONISM

When Will the Rapture Occur?

Once a person's belief about the end times has settled on premillennialism, the next question they must answer for themselves is, "When will the rapture occur, before or after the great tribulation?"

Two distinct groups offer answers.

- Christian who believe in *pre*tribulational premillennialism believe that the rapture will occur *before* the great tribulation.

- Christian who believe in *post*tribulational premillennialism believe that the rapture will occur *after* the great tribulation.

In other words, pretrib theology holds that believers won't suffer through the tribulation while postrib theology maintains that believers will. Both believe the rapture will happen, but they differ on the timing of it.

Now, my belief in pretribulational premillennialism isn't predicated upon my desire to escape suffering. (Jesus assured us all that suffering was part of the deal anyway. See John 16:33.) My belief is predicated upon what the Bible says, even though it wasn't always that way, so to speak.

As I mentioned, I once held to posttribulational belief, largely due to a few verses that seemed fairly straightforward to me upon first reading, like Matthew 24:22: "And except those days should be shortened, there should no flesh be saved: but for the elect's sake those days shall be shortened." In reading that verse, it's clear that the elect are present during the time of the great tribulation. Consequently, the rapture must happen *after* the tribulation.

But at the base of that innocent belief is a broad assumption: I'm one of the elect. Of course, that's what anyone who believes in that kind of election says: "Whoever is in the elect, it must be me." But I define "the elect" much differently now, and that was part of the changing of my belief from posttribulational to pretribulational.

Graphically Representing the Current Views on Rapture

The following graphical representations of rapture views are all subsections of premillennialism because only premillennialism sees the rapture as significantly different from the Second Coming. Because premillennialism separates the rapture from the Second Coming, premillennialists must decide on the timing of the rapture. Pre-Tribulational and Post-Tribulational views are the dominant views, while the Mid-Tribulational and Partial Tribulational views are growing in popularity in recent years. The Pre-Wrath view is a modification of the Mid-Tribulational view.

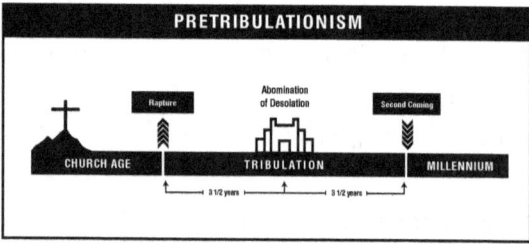

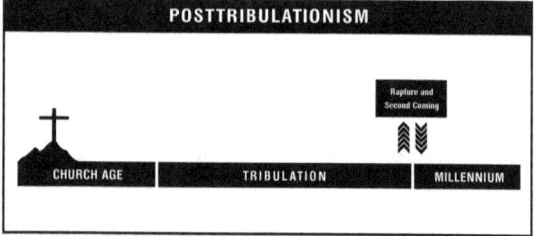

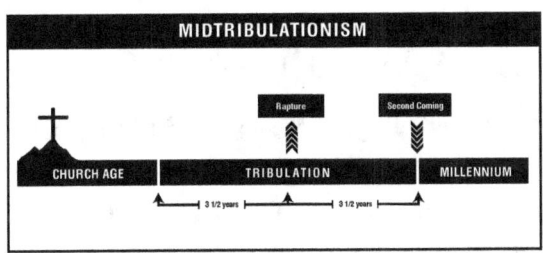

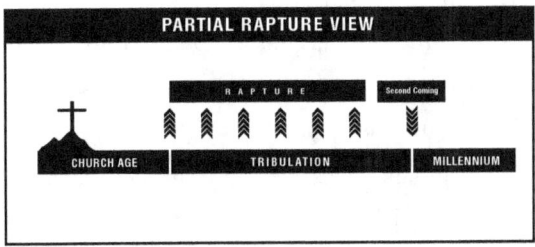

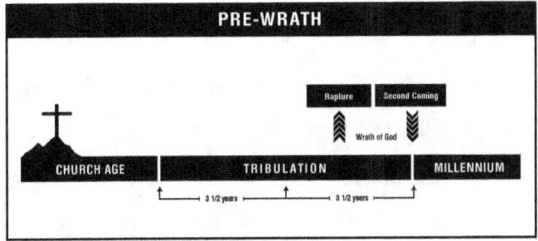

Are the Rapture and the Second Coming the Same Thing?

As with all good theology, right belief stems from right thinking, and right thinking comes from clearly understanding what the Bible says, and always with the eye-opening assistance of the Holy Spirit. We must keep defining what we mean by certain terms and phrases to ensure that we're not holding onto cultural assumptions or incorrect biblical positions.

For instance, what's going to happen when the Lord returns? Does the rapture happen then? Is his second coming the same as the rapture? When good students of the Word are asked about the Lord's return, their response ought to be, "Which return?"

I am convinced that the rapture is *not* the same thing as the second coming.

My reasons for such belief are based on two aspects of both events: imminence and visibility.

Imminence means "happening very soon," and visibility simply means "able to be seen."

Is the Second Coming Imminent?

Let's consider the question of imminence first. Pause for a moment and answer this question: Is the second coming of Christ imminent? In other words, could he return at the very moment you're reading these words?

A vast majority of Christians would probably answer yes. After all, "But of that day and hour knoweth no man, no, not the angels of heaven, but my Father only." (Matthew 24:36). Yet if we look closely at a few verses before that, we'll read why the second coming is *not* imminent.

> "For then shall be great tribulation, such as was not since the beginning of the world to this time, no, nor ever shall be. And except those days should be shortened, there should no flesh be saved: but for the elect's sake those days shall be shortened. . . .

Immediately after the tribulation of those days shall the sun be darkened, and the moon shall not give her light, and the stars shall fall from heaven, and the powers of the heavens shall be shaken'" (Matthew 24:21–22, 29).

Matthew 24:30 then explicitly describes Christ's second coming: "And then shall appear the sign of the Son of man in heaven: and then shall all the tribes of the earth mourn, and they shall see the Son of man coming in the clouds of heaven with power and great glory."

Let me remind you that this is Jesus talking about himself. He's telling his first-century audience about what's going to happen many millennia from then. He's saying that a great tribulation of terrible suffering will occur, and then he's going to return to put a stop to it. In fact, the suffering will be so bad that he's going to shorten the days or else *no one would survive it*. That's terrifying.

In deciding whether or not the second coming

is imminent, you must ask yourself, "Has something so terrible happened in history that the days needed to be shortened so that at least some people would survive it?" The answer is no, despite what some well-meaning Christians may say.

Such Christians believe that the book of Revelation has been fulfilled, if not in whole, then at least in part, and at least enough for them to believe that the second coming of Christ is imminent. They will argue that the Antichrist spoken of in Revelation was actually Nero or Domitian, both first-century Roman emperors. They will argue that the great tribulation occurred when Rome destroyed the temple in Jerusalem in AD 70. While that destruction was certainly horrible, there was zero risk that *all* the flesh of humanity would cease had the Romans kept up their work. In other words, the great tribulation has yet to occur.

Requirements for the Second Coming

If you read your Bible literally, a second coming is *not* imminent because its stated requirements have yet to be fulfilled. According to the Bible, the second coming must be preceded by:

- A seven-year period of tribulation.
- The existence of an Antichrist.
- The Antichrist setting himself up to be worshipped as a God at the midpoint of the tribulation.
- The necessity to have the Mark of the Beast in order to buy or sell.
- A cataclysmic, ecosystem-affecting, global event.
- The sun ceasing to shine (causing the moon to go dark) at the tribulations's end.

Then and only then will the sign of the Son of Man shall appear and the second coming happen.

Furthermore, the book of Revelation sets a specific timeline for some events that precede Christ's second coming. Multiple times, John writes about two witnesses on Jesus's behalf who will serve him for 1,260 days leading up to his second coming. In other words, once these two witnesses make themselves known, we can actually put the day of the Lord's return *on our calendars*. But we can't do that now because *none* of the events previously listed have occurred. Consequently, the second coming is *not* imminent.

Is the Rapture Imminent?

Yes! Unlike the second coming, the rapture could occur even as you're reading these words. Time and again, Paul speaks to the rapture's near possibility for every believer.

No certain circumstances have to occur before the rapture. But if you want to be included in the rapture, you'll need to have believed on Christ for your salvation.

Is the Second Coming Visible?

In addition to imminence, the aspect of visibility must also be addressed when differentiating the second coming from the rapture. The second coming *is* visible. That is, when it happens, it will be visually witnessed.

Matthew 24:26–27 couldn't be any clearer about that fact: "Wherefore if they shall say unto you, Behold, he is in the desert; go not forth: behold, he is in the secret chambers; believe it not. For as the lightning cometh out of the east, and shineth even unto the west; so shall also the coming of the Son of man be." Together, those verses are essentially saying, "When Jesus comes back, you won't have to look for him. His return won't be a secret. The second coming will be very visible—the most incredible news story of all time."

Is the Rapture Visible?

The Apostle Paul answers this question: "Behold, I shew you a mystery; We shall not all sleep, but we shall all be changed, *In a moment, in the twinkling of an eye*, at the last trump: for the trumpet shall sound, and the dead shall be raised incorruptible, and we shall be changed" (1 Corinthians 15:51-52, emphasis added).

The rapture is sometimes described as "the invisible rapture" because of the rapidity with which it will occur. If we were witnesses to the rapture and our eyes could perceive in super slow-motion, we *might see* what's happening. But the reality of what will happen will occur so quickly that not even the world's best photographer could capture it on film. In an instant faster than a snapshot, the world will suddenly see that a good number of people from around the world are no longer around.

So are the rapture and the second coming the same thing? No! If the rapture is imminent but won't be visible and the second coming will be visible but isn't imminent, we must conclude that the rapture and the second coming are different events. If that hasn't made the case for you, yet one more question may help.

Where Will the People of God Gather At His Return?

1 Thessalonians 4:17 says, "Then we which are alive and remain shall be caught up together with them in the clouds, to meet the Lord in the air: and so shall we ever be with the Lord." This Scripture is pretty clear that we will meet the Lord in the air.

However, Zechariah 14:3-5 says, "Then shall the Lord go forth, and fight against those nations, as when he fought in the day of battle. And his feet shall stand in that day upon the mount of Olives, which is before Jerusalem on the east, and *the mount of Olives shall cleave* in the midst thereof toward the east and toward the west, and there shall be a very great valley; and half of the mountain shall remove toward the north, and half of it toward the south. And ye shall flee to the valley of the mountains ..." (emphasis added).

When I first preached the message that this short book is based upon, I left the following day to go to Israel. While there, I stood on the Mount of Olives. Much to no one's surprise, the Mount did not "cleave," or split into two pieces, while I stood upon it, proving that I'm not the Messiah. But when Jesus returns, he will return at the Mount of Olives. When his feet touch that ground, that mountain will split. Without a doubt, we'll know it's him.

A vast and ancient cemetery still exists on the Mount of Olives. A small tomb inscribed with "Zechariah" even leads us to believe that the Minor Prophet who wrote the book that bears his name is buried there. In fact, the Jewish people consider this cemetery to be the most prestigious burial ground in the world. Why? Because of the verses we just covered. The Jews believe that the Mount of Olives is where their Messiah will return. When he returns they will follow Zechariah's admonition to "flee to the valley of the mountains."

That valley is the Valley of Jehoshaphat, also known as the Valley of Decision, where the judgment of the nations will take place. Believing that there will be a long line for that judgment, the Jewish people are essentially just ensuring that they will be at the front of the line when that time comes. So they long to be buried in the cemetery on the Mount of Olives.

For us, a question still remains: will believers meet Christ in the air or at the Mount of Olives? Again, the answer is clear when you separate the rapture from the second coming. Believers will meet Christ in the air when the rapture occurs. Those who are still around for the great tribulation will meet him at the Valley of Decision after the second coming has occurred.

To summarize what we've so far discussed, the rapture and the second coming are not the same thing because:

- The rapture is imminent and invisible. It could happen right now "in the twinkling of an eye." The rapture will also take place "in the air" around the globe.

- The second coming is not imminent but will be highly visible. Certain prerequisites must occur which have yet to occur, but when the second coming happens, there will be no doubt that it has happened. The second coming will take place at a very particular geographical location: the Mount of Olives in Jerusalem.

Will the Rapture Really Occur?

Because I preach and teach on this topic, people will often say, "That rapture stuff is just pie-in-the-sky, wishful thinking." But if that were true, why would Paul encourage believers to "comfort one another" with the future occurrence of the rapture? Because the church will be removed from suffering during "the Day of the Lord," a phrase we'll discuss more in depth soon enough.

Another argument I often hear is, "I've never read anything about the rapture in the gospels or the Old Testament. It's just Paul who talks about it." My rebuttal is blunt: "Then wouldn't that be verification of a pretribulational rapture?" This answer is sometimes met with a blank stare.

The Old Testament doesn't speak directly to the Church because the Church, according to Paul, is a "mystery." The Bible wouldn't reveal specifics about a mystery before the proper time. But when the mystery of the Church is revealed *after* Pentecost (i.e., *after* the gospels), *then* the further mysteries of the Church may be revealed—like how it's all going to end for this "new thing" that is the Body of Christ. Paul reveals that answer: "Then we which are alive and remain shall be caught up together with them in the clouds, to meet the Lord in the air: and so shall we ever be with the Lord" (1 Thessalonians 4:17).

The rapture will really occur.

CHAPTER 2

MY THEOLOGICAL JOURNEY

I've always been a premillennialist, but I haven't always been a pretribulational premillennialist. My beliefs about this changed because of the overwhelming evidence of Scripture. Of the many verses that speak to the rapture and the second coming, I find 1 Thessalonians 4:17–18 to be the clearest and the most encouraging: "Then we which are alive and remain shall be *caught up* together with them in the clouds, to meet the Lord in the air: and so shall we ever be with the Lord. Wherefore comfort one another with these words." (emphasis added).

As one who always attempts to read the Bible literally, I realized that I needed some kind of rapture theology because of those two short words in the middle of that passage: "caught up." English translations of the Bible don't include the word "rapture," but Latin translations do. In Latin, "caught up" is *rapturo*. If you still don't want to call it a rapture, call it a "catching up." Regardless of what you call it, the Apostle Paul says that we will all be "caught up" or "snatched up" together. According to the Bible, a "catching up" in the air is an inevitability. That was step one in the re-creation of my rapture theology.

The beginning of Paul's second letter to the Thessalonians revealed the next step. In fact, these verses are what caused me to move from posttrib to pretrib belief. To begin that letter, Paul wrote, "Now we beseech you, brethren, *by the coming of our Lord Jesus Christ, and by our gathering together unto him*" (2 Thessalonians 2:1, emphasis added).

When the Bible talks about the Lord's return, what's a good student of the Word supposed to ask? *Which return are we talking about? The rapture or the second coming?* Thankfully, Paul offers a hint: "by our gathering unto him." That sounds an awful lot like being "caught up together," which he had written in his first letter that was sent to the same church. Paul is talking about the rapture.

He continues, "That ye be not soon shaken in mind, or be troubled, neither by spirit, nor by word, nor by letter as from us, as that the day of Christ is at hand" (1 Thessalonians 2:2). Paul uses such a strong word for "shaken" that he's almost describing the effects of an earthquake. In essence, he's saying, "I don't want you to have an earthquake of your soul by believing that the Day of the Lord is at hand."

But what sense does that make? Wouldn't early believers ardently desire that the Day of the Lord be near? Don't they want to be raptured—caught up together—with Jesus in the air?

The early believers in the Thessalonian church may have received a forged letter proclaiming something else: that "the Day of the Lord" is already here and no rapture will take you out. The believers at Thessalonica would have every right to be "shaken" about Paul's words regarding the Day of the Lord because this forged letter said something that made it seem as if Paul had changed his mind. And if Paul was flip-flopping on his beliefs, why would those believers choose to keep trusting his words? Thessalonian believers would have been questioning themselves with, "Just how many more 'oops, I was wrong' letters are we going to keep receiving from Paul?"

That's why Paul makes sure to mention that this particular letter was written by him. 2 Thessalonians 3:17 says, "The salutation of Paul *with mine own hand*, which is the token of every epistle: so I write" (emphasis added). What Paul's really trying to tell the Thessalonian believers is, "Don't believe the lie of that forged letter. I'm sticking to my story. The Day of the Lord is coming. But it hasn't happened yet."

Let's answer some more questions about pretribulationalism before I continue my theological journey.

CHAPTER 3

MORE QUESTIONS ABOUT PRETRIBULATIONISM

What is The Day of the Lord?

Do you know how the Bible describes "The Day of the Lord"?

Once you read through these verses, you'll understand even more why the first-century believers at Thessalonica would have been having soul-level earthquakes at just the hint that the Day of the Lord would be happening any time soon:

- "Howl ye; for the day of the Lord is at hand; it shall come as a destruction from the Almighty" (Isaiah 13:6).

- "Behold, the day of the Lord cometh, cruel both with wrath and fierce anger, to lay the land desolate: and he shall destroy the sinners thereof out of it" (Isaiah 13:9).

- The prophet Jeremiah speaks to God: "Thou hast called as in a solemn day my terrors round about, so that in the day of the Lord's anger none escaped nor remained: those that I have swaddled and brought up hath mine enemy consumed" (Lamentations 2:22).

- "For the day is near, even the day of the Lord is near, a cloudy day; it shall be the time of the heathen" (Ezekiel 30:3).

- "Blow ye the trumpet in Zion, and sound an alarm in my holy mountain: let all the inhabitants of the land tremble: for the day of the Lord cometh, for it is nigh at hand" (Joel 2:1).

I could cite half-a-dozen more verses, but you get the bleak picture.

Nowhere in Scripture will you find a passage that

describes the Day of the Lord as "a blessed time of joy that we should look forward to." Rather, the Day of the Lord is always described in an alarming fashion, which makes sense.

The Day of the Lord is God's terrible and total judgment made real.

What Has to Happen Before the Day of the Lord Occurs?

Paul is very clear that two particular criteria must be met *before* the Day of the Lord will happen. 2 Thessalonians 2:3–5 says, "Let no man deceive you by any means: for that day shall not come, *except there come a falling away first, and that man of sin be revealed, the son of perdition*; Who opposeth and exalteth himself above all that is called God, or that is worshipped; so that he as God sitteth in the temple of God, shewing himself that he is God. Remember ye not, that, when I was yet with you, I told you these things?" (emphasis added).

So, in order to ascertain if the Day of the Lord has happened or will happen in the near future, we must ask ourselves two questions:

Has a "falling away" occurred?

Has the "man of sin" been revealed?

The simple answer to both of those questions is no, but let's see what the Bible says.

Has a "Falling Away" Occurred?

The Greek word Paul uses for "falling away" is *apostasia*, the word from which derives the English word "apostasy." The traditional interpretation of the apostasy Paul's speaking about is that it hasn't occurred as evidenced by verses like 1 Thessalonians 1:7–8: "So that ye were ensamples (examples) to all that believe in Macedonia and Achaia. For from you sounded out the word of the Lord not only in Macedonia and Achaia, but also in every place your faith to God-ward is spread abroad; so that we need not to speak any thing."

That doesn't sound like a "falling away," does it? In fact, it sounds like the exact opposite. The incredible growth of the first-century church reveals the same fact. In the time when the Thessalonians were reading Paul's letters, the church was adding hundreds to its ranks on any given day.

Personally, I believe we've mistranslated *apostasia*. While the traditional view is by no means wrong, my very literal translation of that word opens this section of Scripture to encompass a secondary meaning that takes nothing away from the traditional perspective.

Stasis means "standing." If you place your feet firmly on the ground with the intent to not be moved, you're in stasis. *Apo* means "to take away." So, *apo-stasis* means "to take away a standing." The traditional view interprets this as "a falling away," which is true enough. People are going to leave their places of commitment and they're going to fall away.

But could it also be true that if you're "caught up," you're "away from your standing"? I actually think what Paul is saying here is, "The Day of the Lord will not come until you're not standing (*apo-stasis*) anymore because you've been taken from where you're standing. You've been caught up—raptured."

Regardless of your interpretation of *apostasia*, the main concerning matter is that *the rapture hasn't occurred yet*. Paul is saying that the Day of the Lord won't happen until *after* the *apostasis*.

But what about that second event that has to happen before the Day of the Lord occurs?

Has the "Man of Sin" Been Revealed?

As you likely already guessed, the "man of sin" is the Antichrist. And even though many well-meaning Christians have named certain people as the Antichrist (even since the first century), the "man of sin" has yet to be revealed.

For instance, Paul lived when Nero ruled Rome. If Paul wrote that the man of sin hasn't been revealed, then he's implicitly telling his readers, "Despite what you may think, Nero isn't the Antichrist." Furthermore, no person has *ever* set themselves up in God's temple proclaiming to be God. Despite the many evil people that have existed throughout the centuries, no person has yet to fulfill all of the Bible's prophesies concerning the Antichrist. Consequently, the "man of sin" has yet to be revealed.

So, the Day of the Lord was not upon the believers at Thessalonica because no great falling away had occurred and the man of sin hadn't been revealed. Therefore, Paul encouraged those Christians that they "be not soon shaken in mind." The great and terrible Day of the Lord was not happening, nor would it anytime soon.

Why I Believe in Pretribulationism

If my study into what "the Day of the Lord" really means didn't fully sway me from postrib to pretrib belief, 1 Thessalonians 1:10 cemented the change. In that verse, Paul tells the believers in Thessalonica to "Wait for his Son from heaven, whom he raised from the dead, even Jesus, which delivered us from the wrath to come."

It's that last clause that good students of the Bible will question themselves about: "What is this wrath to come that He's delivering us from?" The easy answer is hell. Jesus delivered us from the wrath of hell that is to come, right? Well, yes and no. That statement is certainly true, but not in the context of what Paul's talking about in his first letter to the Thessalonians.

Always allow the Bible to interpret itself. Multiple verses in the book of Revelation describe "the wrath to come." Revelation 6:16–17 reveals that all the people of the world will say "to the mountains and the rocks, Fall on us, and hide us from the face of him that sitteth on the throne, and from the wrath of the Lamb: For the great day of his wrath is come;

and who shall be able to stand?'" Clearly, that takes place during the tribulation.

But how can I be so certain that "the wrath to come" that Paul describes is the same "wrath to come" John speaks about in Revelation? Because the only other places in the Bible that talk about "the wrath to come" are about "the Day of the Lord." And as we know now, that will *not* be a good day for those here who must suffer through it.

But, praise God, Jesus has "delivered us from the wrath to come."

What wrath is that? The Day of the Lord wrath.

Christians will be raptured *before* the Day of the Lord occurs.

We will all be gone "in a twinkling of an eye," *pretribulationally*.

You can debate who the Antichrist may be, or how to buy or sell merchandise without taking the Mark of the Beast, or how you'll live under a global government—but those are all hypothetical, moot questions for the Christian. They're interesting issues to consider, but they ultimately won't matter to you.

You won't be on the earth to experience them.

CONCLUSION

There remains one last issue that caused me to move from postribulational to pretribulational belief: the prophesied return of the Jews to their homeland in Israel. Zechariah 8:1–6 says,

> Again the word of the Lord of hosts came to me, saying, Thus saith the Lord of hosts; I was jealous for Zion with great jealousy, and I was jealous for her with great fury. Thus saith the Lord; I am returned unto Zion, and will dwell in the midst of Jerusalem: and Jerusalem shall be called a city of truth; and the mountain of the Lord of hosts the holy mountain. Thus saith the Lord of hosts; There shall yet old men and old women dwell in the streets of Jerusalem, and every man with his staff in his hand for very age. And

> the streets of the city shall be full of boys and girls playing in the streets thereof. Thus saith the Lord of hosts; If it be marvellous in the eyes of the remnant of this people in these days, should it also be marvellous in mine eyes? saith the Lord of hosts.

In this passage, the minor prophet Zechariah speaks about what many other passages in the Bible speak about: that the Jewish people will return to Israel in due time and that their return will happen *before* the Day of the Lord.

Since the destruction of the Temple in Jerusalem in AD 72, the Jews have been scattered across the globe. But just within the last few years, the number of Jews living in Israel has finally increased to more than the number of Jews living elsewhere. New York City and Florida used to have more Jewish residents than Israel, but that's no longer the case.

Even more intriguing to me than those facts are the personal stories I've heard from Jewish people who are willingly choosing to move back to Israel.

I've asked them, "Don't you watch the news? They're trying to kill you over there. Why wouldn't you choose to stay in the states where you and your family can be safe and happy?" Their replies are almost always the same: "I don't know why. Something's just drawing me to Israel. I can't really tell you what it is."

I know what *it* is: God.

For the last century, God has been drawing his people back to Israel for their restoration. And if God is going to be so precise in that act, we can certainly trust his Word that the Day of the Lord is soon to follow. The "Day of Jacob's trouble" is coming where two witnesses and 144,000 Jewish apostles will attest to Jesus's messiahship. God's people will eventually mourn whom they once pierced. A great battle will ensue as the Lord returns *at the Mount of Olives* to fight one last fight on behalf of his chosen people. The mountain will split in two, judgment of the nations will commence, and then his kingdom—the millennium—will begin.

When I see the ancient words of Scripture aligning with present-day trends, like the massive reverse exodus of the Jewish people back to Israel, I believe even more firmly that God will do exactly what he said he will do. Consequently, if he tells me that we'll be delivered from the day of wrath that is to come, I can have full confidence that *we will be delivered from the day of wrath that is to come*. I don't suffer from soul-level earthquakes or fear of the unknown future because the Lord has told us what to expect.

In other words, I believe in pretribulational premillennialism.

I look forward to the day when the trumpets shall sound, the Lord shall descend, the dead in Christ shall rise, and we who are alive and remain will be caught up together with Him to meet the Lord in the air.

Allow these words to comfort you, and choose to comfort one another with them as well.

Dispensational Publishing House is striving to become the go-to source for Bible-based materials from the dispensational perspective.

Our goal is to provide high-quality doctrinal and worldview resources that make dispensational theology accessible to people at all levels of understanding.

Visit our blog regularly to read informative articles from both known and new writers.

And please let us know how we can better serve you.

Dispensational Publishing House, Inc.
PO Box 3181
Taos, NM 87571

Call us toll free 844-321-4202

www.ingramcontent.com/pod-product-compliance
Lightning Source LLC
Chambersburg PA
CBHW071545080526
44588CB00011B/1807